Outside/Inside

Also by Gila Manolson:

The Magic Touch: A Jewish Approach to Relationships

Head to Heart: What to Know Before Dating and Marriage

Outside/Inside

A Fresh Look at *Tzniut*

by Gila Manolson

TARGUM/FELDHEIM

First edition published 1997
Revised and expanded edition published 2005

ISBN: 1-56871-341-x

Published by:
TARGUM PRESS, INC.
22700 W. Eleven Mile Rd., Southfield, MI 48034
E-mail: targum@netvision.net.il
Fax: 888-298-9992
www.targum.com

Distributed by:
FELDHEIM PUBLISHERS
208 Airport Executive Park, Nanuet, NY 10954

Printing plates: "Frank," Jerusalem

Printed in Israel

Dedication

To my children:

Chananya Baruch
Elyashiv Devir
Yair Simcha
Temima Sara
Emuna Rachel
Ayelet Ora
and
Yisrael Leib

Your coming into the world taught me about the potential within us all.

RABBI ZEV LEFF
Rabbi of Moshav Matityahu
Rosh Hayeshiva Yeshiva Gedola Matisyahu

D.N. Modiin 71917 Tel: 08-976-1138 Fax: 08-976-5326

I know Mrs. Gila Manolson as a woman of valor, the wife of a serious Torah scholar, capable of expressing Torah ideas and ideals in a manner that can impress and inspire both those unfamiliar with the Torah way of life and those already committed to it.

In this work, *Outside/Inside*, Mrs. Manolson masterfully conveys one of the many facets of the Torah concept of *tzniut* (modesty), giving readers an intellectual and emotional taste of this important foundation of Torah living.

"God has told you, humanity, what is good; and what does the Lord require of you but to do justly, love kindness, and walk in *tzniut* with your God" (Micah 6:8). *Tzniut* is the perfection of justice and kindness, for it transforms these practical needs of a functioning society into Godly pursuits. Whenever there exists an internal dimension that could be forgotten, we modestly cover the externals, making them into a vehicle for transmitting inner beauty. The message is that there is more here than meets the eye — that the essence is spiritual. Thus, modesty applies not only to men and women, but to holy objects such as those in the Mishkan (Sanctuary); not only to dress, but also to actions, speech, and thought.

I highly recommend reading *Outside/Inside* and am confident that it will greatly aid in promoting true *tzniut* among the Jewish people.

With Torah blessings,

Rabbi Zev Leff
Moshav Matityahu

We live in a generation searching for its own identity. The "isms" that once assuaged the thirst for meaningful self-definition often seem no longer relevant or applicable. While the Torah way of life has an unrivaled radiance and depth, it is unquestionably under-explored by those on the "outside" and often undervalued by those on the "inside." A major cause is the stereotypes people have of the Torah lifestyle — none of which is more damaging and untrue than those surrounding *tzniut* (modesty).

Gila Manolson has, once again, presented us with a book that will do more than pry open closed minds. *Outside/Inside* provides insight and inspiration to those of us who share her values but have not explored beneath the surface. The beauty and clarity of her writing is a rare gift.

I have known Gila for many years. The living example she provides in her sincere pursuit of truth, her empathy for her fellow seekers, and her striving to integrate genuine *tzniut* into every aspect of her life, makes her authorship of this book most appropriate.

Tziporah Heller

Tziporah Heller
Neve Yerushalayim

Contents

Preface

Several years ago, I wrote a book called *The Magic Touch: A Jewish Approach to Relationships* (originally subtitled *A Candid Look at the Jewish Approach to Relationships*). Addressed primarily to young adults, it offered a practical rationale for refraining from all physical contact with the opposite sex before marriage — being "*shomer negiah.*" The book received many positive responses (at least from females — one told me, "You're famous among girls and infamous among our boyfriends!") and has been widely read among newcomers to Judaism. Many schools and programs have since asked me to address their students on this topic.

On one such occasion, a young woman approached me after class. "Everything you've said makes so much sense, and I really want to be *shomer negiah*. But" she sighed unhappily, "there's one problem."

"What?" I asked.

"I'm afraid my boyfriend will break up with me."

That's when it hit me: It's hard to be *shomer negiah* if you lack self-worth and the inner strength it creates. And this lack affects not only relationships but other areas of life as well.

To address this problem, I wrote *Outside/Inside*. Since then, I have more to say on the subject — hence this new revised and expanded edition.

If *The Magic Touch* challenged your beliefs and lifestyle, *Outside/Inside* is likely to challenge you on an even more essential level. More threatening than changing your behavior in relationships is the prospect of rethinking who you are. Yet a deep exploration of your identity and its implications is what this book asks of you. I hope you will approach it with an open mind, and face the challenge.

G.M.
Jerusalem

Acknowledgments

I would like to thank the following people from the bottom of my heart:

My teacher Tziporah Heller (author of *More Precious than Pearls: Selected Insights into the Qualities of the Ideal Woman* and *Our Bodies/Our Souls: A Jewish Perspective on Feminine Spirituality*), for giving me the essential understanding of *tzniut* which underlies not only this book but my life;

Rabbi Zev Leff, Rabbi Dr. Natan Lopes-Cardozo, and again, Rebbetzin Heller, for generously taking time out of their busy lives to review the manuscript;

My very special and wonderful friends: Rhonda Halpern, Yehudis Golshevsky, Dina Coopersmith, Devorah Fastag, and Chaya Rivka Jessel, of blessed memory (who provided the book's title), for their indispensable comments and critiques; Rachel Averick, for supplying an important missing piece; Shaina Buchwald and Leah Shachter, for providing the impetus for some major overhauling; Simi Peters, for reviewing the original draft of the chapter on individuality; Batya Friedman, for (along with everything else) her exceptional depth and insight in identifying what more needed to be said; and Marina Goodman (author of *Why Should I Stand Behind the Mechitzah When I Could Be a Prayer Leader? The Traditional Jewish Response for the Contemporary Jewish Woman*), for her tremendously helpful suggestions and continual intellectual and emotional support;

Shlomo Aharon Fenster, Mordechai McKenney, Justin Levitz, and Rachel Templeton, for their sensitive and tuned-in comments;

Ro'i Furer, for suggesting some important organizational changes, and for his ongoing encouragement;

Rabbi Marc Kujawski and Devorah Nov, authors of the article "'*Ayeka?*': *Mekom HaOtentiut BaMachshava HaYehudit* ['Where Are You?': The Place of Authenticity in Jewish Thought]" (included in the book *Kanfei Ruach: P'rakim BeZehut, Yetzira, VeYachasei Guf-Nefesh-Ruach* [Wings of Spirit: Reflections on Identity, Creativity, and the Relationship between Body, Mind, and Soul], which I look forward to reading); Sarah Schneider, author of *Kabbalistic Writings on the Nature of Masculine and Feminine*; Shaina Sara Handelman, Ph.D., author of the articles "The Concept of 'Modesty': A Torah Perspective" (in *The Modern Jewish Woman: A Unique Perspective*) and "The Paradoxes of Privacy" (in *Sh'ma: A Journal of Jewish Responsibility*, November 10, 1978); Rabbi Moshe Meiselman, author of *Jewish Woman in Jewish Law*; Wendy Shalit, author of *A Return to Modesty: Discovering the Lost Virtue*; Malka Touger, author of *Just My Style: A Tznius Reader for Teens*; Rebbetzin Yitti Neustadt, Rabbi Raymond Breyda, and once again, Rebbetzin Heller, for their audiotapes on *tzniut*, which have deeply enriched my understanding; and Shprintzee Herskovitz, for a beautiful idea from her book *Rays of the Sun*;

The many program and seminary directors who have allowed me the privilege and pleasure of sharing these ideas and others with their audiences;

My students from here, there, and everywhere over the years, for nurturing my mind and soul with their questions and appreciation;

A certain friend, for providing insight into what she called (while unknowingly possessing it) the "lost art";

And finally, my incredibly wonderful, devoted husband, Avraham, for being a constant role model of *tzniut*, a source of valuable input, and a bedrock of support and love.

May Hashem continue to bless them all with the ability and energy to make a difference.

Introduction

Since age 22, when I began exploring Judaism, I've spent a lot of time talking with people about something called *tzniut* (pronounced tz'neeOOT). *Tzniut* translates loosely and rather inadequately as "modesty" and is inevitably one of the first issues a newcomer to Judaism confronts. Initially I was an adversary, challenging the proponents of *tzniut* to explain why a woman would necessarily become more spiritual upon trading in tight jeans and a tank top for a skirt and sleeves. In time, however, I became an advocate, attempting to communicate — to those who stood where I once had — the power of an idea and practice I was struggling to make my own. But it was not quite a new idea — for the more I learned, the more I felt I was rediscovering something I already knew.

Tzniut may be new and foreign to you, or you may already be somewhat familiar with it. If you're in the latter group, chances are you subscribe to some commonly held beliefs about *tzniut*. The first is that *tzniut* is a dress code. The second is that it is only for women. The third is that the reason for *tzniut*, ironically, has nothing to do with women but with men. Males, it has been observed, have trouble focusing on spiritual matters when around less than modestly clad females. Given the impracticality of asking them to don blinders, the rationale goes, Judaism instead tells women to be good sports and cover up.

It's not hard to see where these beliefs have come from. Dress is a strong focus of *tzniut*; *tzniut* is stressed more among females than males; and women are indeed held responsible (within limits) for the effect their attire has upon men, just as all Jews are responsible for one another. Still, viewing *tzniut* as a restriction of women to protect men is a tragic reduction of a profound concept. As a result, perhaps the most dynamic agent of personal and social change is belittled or, at best, ignored.

We can scarcely afford this loss, for much needs to change. So many in our society suffer ongoing unhappiness — whether a throbbing pain born of outright failure (most often in relationships) or just a haunting feeling that beneath our apparent success, something is missing. For despite the proliferation of self-help books, tapes, and e-mails, most of us haven't yet acquired deep, stable, spiritual self-knowledge — and it's hard to find happiness when we haven't found ourselves.

Yet we can. And today, *tzniut* is truly a light in the darkness. For *tzniut* is infinitely more than what we wear — it's who we are. It's the potential within every one of us, male and female, and Judaism enjoins us all to actualize it. *Tzniut* is the key to all spiritual growth and therefore to a healthy society. Rather than restricting, *tzniut* is, in the most profound sense, liberating.

Anything spiritual is difficult to capture in words. *Tzniut*, too, can be truly understood only through witnessing it, or better, living it. Still, I hope my words, however limited, will dispel misconceptions and deepen our appreciation of a fundamental Jewish idea — one that, if taken to heart, can revolutionize our lives.

CHAPTER ONE

Your Body/Yourself

Usually, we see things as they appear on the surface. We look at an old tree and see its trunk and branches. We look at a tomb and see cold granite. We look at the Kotel (Western Wall, in Jerusalem's Old City) and see ancient stones.

Yet if we look more deeply, things are more than what they seem. The gnarled tree offers a stirring affirmation of timeless endurance. The Hebrew-inscribed tombstone in a neglected Polish cemetery represents a soul crying out from a lost world. The same object can even be "read" in different ways: The Kotel symbolizes the Jewish people's fall from glory, or — with fresh greenery bursting out of its cracks — proclaims that same people's rebirth in its land.

We too can be seen superficially, as objects — or as people radiating a message. To a large extent, it depends how we relate to our outer selves — our bodies.

More than Skin-Deep

Judaism teaches that God wants us to perceive each other in depth. God therefore empowered the first man and woman to see each other's outer and inner selves as one. When Adam gazed at Eve's body, he saw her mind, heart, and spirit. As Eve appreciated Adam's exterior, she appreciated his essence. Humans saw each other in their entirety, with outside and inside inseparable.

But this idyllic state was short-lived. A fatal error destroyed humanity's vision, and we fell into a world of confusion and illusion. The body now assumed an independent identity, its glare obscuring the inner self. And that's how we often view one another today.

Imagine running into someone you haven't seen for some time and discovering that she has had plastic surgery and gained (or lost) 100 pounds. It would probably be difficult to relate to her as the same person. The outside blocks our vision of the inside.

Originally, when man and woman saw through each other, outside to inside, nakedness posed no obstacle to perception. Today, it does. Every society has therefore embraced Adam and Eve's solution: clothing.

To understand what clothes mean to us, look at how we expect different creatures to dress. Animals, for example, aren't expected to wear anything. No one I know has ever gasped, "That dog is walking the streets stark naked! What ever happened to decency?!"

Humans, however, do wear clothes. Yet our "dress code" depends upon age. You would probably find it adorable if your neighbor's toddler innocently showed up at your front door straight from the bath. If the same child repeated that behavior at age 10, I suspect you'd be less amused. And if the visitor were an adult, you'd call the police.

Why the difference?

Simple: The farther removed a person is from an animal, the more we expect that person to wear. A dog can trot around au naturel without being considered "naked," since (animal lovers, please forgive me) it is essentially a physical being, governed by senses and instincts. A baby is similar — it cannot yet make moral decisions, delay gratification, or put another's needs before its own. Thus, while we call it "naked" in recognition of its inherent humanity, no one blushes at its bare bottom. A 10-year-old, however, is already (hopefully) way beyond that, and a 20-year-old even more so — which is why an adult who parades around without clothes is not cute, but an exhibitionist.

Clothing likewise reflects "mode." Poolside, for example, it's appropriate to wear very little, because sunning and swimming are physical activities. But you probably wouldn't accept a Nobel Prize in your bathing suit.

Covering yourself is therefore the most fundamental way of saying, "I'm more than a body." The Hebrew word for clothing is *levush*, related to the word *busha*, shame. The body isn't shameful, but being seen as no more than a body *is*. Clothing removes that shame by directing attention past the outside to the inside. It's the first step in asserting our personhood. And the more of our bodies we cover, the less they eclipse who we are.

I read a story (recounted in my book *Head to Heart*) about a female college professor who was set up on a blind date. As she was a bookish intellectual, her date was warned that she might dress primly — but she showed up in a low-cut dress with a thigh-high slit. "Wow!" he blurted out, taken aback. "Your brains don't show at all!"

Women have trouble believing bodies are so distracting. "When I meet a man," insisted a woman in one of my classes, "the first thing I notice is his personality."

I turned to the men in the room. "Guys, when you meet a girl, what's the first thing *you* notice?" Silence — and guilty grins. The fact is that no man sees a woman on the street and thinks, "Is her personality ever a knock-out!"

The more you emphasize your body, the more easily others unconsciously mistake it for your real self.

A friend of mine, newly observant and married, was driving with her uncle.

"Look at your oppressive lifestyle," he argued. "You're covered from head to toe. How can you possibly express your personality in such a sexist society? In the religious world, women are nothing!"

Just then, they passed a billboard advertising a perfume called "Personality." Featured was a barely dressed, provocatively posed woman gazing seductively at her audience, perfume bottle in hand. The caption read, "You can see she has Personality."

My friend shook her head. If that's "expressing your personality," she thought, in whose world are women nothing??

Society has trained us that "if you've got it, flaunt it." The message is: "Look how I look!" But if you move toward concealing rather than revealing, you can make a more powerful statement: "I'm much more than meets the eye. If you want to see the real me, you'll have to look inside."

Reflected Images

But does it matter if others see the real you? "When I go downtown and guys ogle me," a scantily clad woman told me, "I ignore them. It doesn't affect me. I know who I am."

Yet even if you know who you are, how others see you *does* affect you.

In fact, even before anyone sees you, your dress affects how *you* see *yourself* — which is why you wear what you wear. For instance, my friend got all dressed up to take her comprehensive exams for her master's degree. When I jokingly asked her if she had a date with her professor, she replied, "Remember the book *Dress for Success?* Looking my best helps give me the confidence I'll need to *do* my best."

I once came across a book called *How to Marry the Rich* (too late — I was already married). The author advised gold diggers to enter exclusive boutiques and try on the most expensive clothing available. By repeatedly experiencing yourself in thousand-dollar outfits, she explained, you'll come to feel rich, which will give you the air necessary to attract millionaires.

The Torah (Genesis 39:7-12) narrates the story of Joseph's encounter with the wife of the Egyptian officer Potiphar. According to Kabbalistic tradition (Zohar, "*VaYeshev*" 238), she knew that to seduce Joseph, he would first have to dress — and therefore feel — like an immoral Egyptian. But Joseph, too, understood the power of clothing, and resisted her by retaining his Hebrew garb.

Once, in a program in which I was teaching, a participant hotly denied any significance to his attire. He "happened" to be wearing a faded T-shirt, torn jeans, and running shoes, as well as a beard and ponytail. I told him, "If what you wear means nothing to you, come back tomorrow with a short haircut, clean-shaven, and in a three-piece suit." He stuttered and stammered, attempted a weak self-defense, then sheepishly conceded the point.

Let's face it: When you put on clothes, you put on a self-image. And every time you look in the mirror and adjust your outfit, that self-image is strengthened. Even in the privacy of your bedroom, therefore, there are styles you would probably never wear, simply because "they're not you." Indeed, some people's defensiveness in confronting this issue testifies to how tightly their self-image is bound up with their clothing. They know that reconsidering their wardrobe means reconsidering who they want to be.

What's most important, however, is not whether you dress rich or poor, earthy or businesslike. What counts is whether you dress "body" or "person."

But the impact of dress upon your self-image is only the beginning. The minute you hit the street, people respond to the image you're projecting — and you pick up on their response. Sociologists call this "symbolic interactionism": How you dress, how others react to you, and how you see yourself all affect each other, shaping who you become. Your self-image is not merely self-produced. It's constantly formed and reformed through contact with others.

This knowledge is empowering. For by choosing how to present yourself, you can largely ensure that your interactions contribute to the self-image you want.

When my friend Shira was dating her future husband, Avi — a pretty strait-laced yeshiva student — they decided to visit a community of very spiritual ex-hippies for Shabbat. Before sunset, Avi went off to change into Shabbat clothes. To Shira's shock, he emerged in white denim pants, an embroidered Indian shirt, and a rainbow *kippa* [yarmulke]. "In these clothes," he explained, "I'll be seen as one of the '*chevra*' [community] — and because I'll then feel more like one of them, I'll be able to experience Shabbat as they do." Sure enough, before she knew it, someone had thrown his arm around Avi's shoulder and said, "Hey, holy brother, let's go *daven* [pray]!" And she'd never seen him pray — and sing and dance — as he did that Shabbat. By dressing to elicit a certain reaction, he altered his self-image for 24 hours and accessed a different side of his spirituality.

If clothing can make such an impact for one day, think what happens when you dress a particular way for months or years. As time goes on, you become who you appear to be — which may be far different from who you "know you are."

Of course, it helps to resist. If you react to construction workers' catcalls by closing your eyes and reminding yourself, "I am a spiritual being," you stand a better chance of preserving your selfhood than if you live for such attention. Still, slowly but surely, repeated assaults on your dignity erode your sense of self. Knowing who you are can't protect you if your appearance tells the world you don't.

I recently leafed through a book about models who have succumbed to anorexia or bulimia in a desperate attempt to remain marketable by society's current beauty standards. A recurrent theme in interviews with these women was their inner emptiness, their absence of self. It's hard to be healthy inside when you're all about your outside, and what others think of it.

The Relating Game

Bodies are perhaps most distracting in relationships — especially when we start off on the wrong foot by dressing "body" instead of "person."

Judy was visiting her friend Laura, who'd just passed the bar exam. Sifting through Laura's closet, the two were deciding what she should wear to an interview with a prestigious law firm the next morning.

Judy, who'd recently become religious, pulled a miniskirt and tank top from a hanger. "How about this?"

"Are you crazy?" Laura exclaimed. "What female lawyer

would wear that to the office? I want to be taken seriously!"

"But when you go out on a Saturday night, hoping to meet a man with whom you can have a genuine relationship — a man who'll take you seriously — this is what you wear?"

Playing with physical attraction is a temporary ego-booster. And everyone seems to be doing it. But if we would step back and clarify what we want in a relationship, we'd probably present ourselves very differently. Like Laura, we're neither stupid nor shallow. We're confused — about what makes us valuable, who we are, and why we deserve love.

Your body is a beautiful gift from God — but you're so much more.

CHAPTER TWO

Show and Tell

Once you move past identifying yourself by your body, it may seem more "real" to define yourself by what you do: "I'm a great keyboard player," "I'm a Rhodes scholar," or "I'm a successful lawyer." Talents, intelligence, and achievements are certainly legitimate and valuable parts of you — but they're still not your truest identity.

My close friend Jan told me a story that taught me a lot about presenting oneself more authentically.

Jan, then 21, was camping on the Sinai coast with her roommate Sue when a bronzed, rugged-looking soldier approached them. Jan's eyes lit up as she prepared to enter "flirt mode." But then the question hit her: Was the mere appearance of a good-looking guy going to "flip her switch" and turn her into an attention-getter? Could she be so easily manipulated? Irked, she resolved to stay centered within herself and ignore this fellow.

Meanwhile, the soldier introduced himself to Sue as Yoni, and the two began talking. After a while, however, he turned his gaze toward Jan.

"He's a paratrooper," Sue told her, "so I mentioned that you've gone parachuting."

"Just once," Jan said.

Yoni continued talking with Sue but frequently looked over at Jan with obvious interest. When Jan eventually joined the conversation, she was struck by the fact that Yoni wasn't just looking to pick up a girl. He actually possessed considerable refinement and depth.

Several months later, they happened to meet again.

"You know what intrigued me about you?" Yoni told Jan. "Most girls flaunt whatever they have to impress a guy. But you didn't seem to feel the need."

In other words, Yoni was interested not because she had once jumped out of a plane, but because she hadn't used that fact to score points. That led him to believe she must be made of deeper stuff.

We crave attention particularly as teenagers. Unsure who we are, we look to externals for identity. Yet even as adults, many of us persist in defining ourselves, if not by our bodies, clothes, or music, then by "what we do" — our hobbies, careers, or accomplishments. But this still isn't "it." Furthermore, when we look to others (such as friends, teammates, coworkers, or employers) for our self-worth, we make ourselves vulnerable to forces beyond our control — and the results often show.

Years ago, I was passing through Grand Central Station in New York when a very self-assured young man strode by. I thought I recognized him. Unable to resist, I approached him and asked, "Excuse me, were you in the movie *Fame?*"

He smiled broadly and answered, "Yes," basking in his celebrity status. How neat to be famous at his age, I thought.

Years later, in Jerusalem, I met someone who'd been at Manhattan's High School for the Performing Arts when *Fame* (which featured students from that school) was made.

"I knew all those actors," she told me. "They were the most insecure, messed-up, miserable kids you could ever meet."

Fame doesn't have to be negative. Yet pursuing it is dangerous, for you can become addicted to others' appraisals of you. A young woman once told me, "I'm a professional entertainer. After a show, the first thing I have to know is, 'Did they like me?' If they did, I'm elated — if they didn't, I'm depressed. I guess I'm really a professional approval-seeker." And deep down, approval-seekers are rarely happy. For people who act as if "all the world's a stage" seldom look inward and ask, "Will the real me please stand up?"

I heard of someone else in the entertainment industry who became a millionaire at age 25. To mark her "arrival," she bought a Porsche, decorated it with ribbons and streamers, and threw a huge party. The champagne flowed as her friends and coworkers toasted her and showered her with congratulations. At the peak of the celebration, amidst cheering, she sat down in the driver's seat of her new sports car for the first time. Then she put her head down on the steering wheel — and cried. For suddenly it hit her: "Is this all I'm about?"

Other people take longer to wake up. I know a middle-aged man who had always seemed together. But when he lost his job in a recession, his world collapsed and he couldn't function. No one realized how much his self-worth was bound up with his income.

Then there's academic success. A first-year student at my highly competitive university was so driven to excel that he already had an ulcer. Ivy League suicide rates are a tragic testimonial to how, in extreme cases, failure to "make the grade" can feel like failure as a human being.

While the examples above include both sexes, it is males who, when asked, "Who are you?" more often answer with a job title or an account of their worldly conquests. While females become sex objects, men become success objects. Both miss the boat in the voyage to self-discovery.

Career, money, academics, sports, travel, politics, the arts, the social scene — the arenas for "proving oneself" are endless. Yet they all share a common denominator: The status they grant you doesn't do justice to your true self.

CHAPTER THREE

Rebel with a Cause

Let's say that, as rightfully proud as you are of your abilities and achievements, you no longer want to define yourself by them. You know there are more significant pursuits from which to derive self-worth. So you involve yourself in a cause.

The world is full of worthy causes: helping the poor, assisting the handicapped, protecting the environment, defending the abused, and more. All can provide tremendous satisfaction and contribute significantly to your personal growth and sense of self. As someone once wrote, "Service to others is one of the cornerstones of building a good life here on earth." Still, no cause, or even group of causes, can serve as your identity.

I spent some time with the "I am my cause" crowd way back when. Sitting cross-legged on the floor in Lower Manhattan one evening, I listened as a massive anti-nuclear demonstration was planned on Wall Street. I heard (and shared) the organizers' disdain for investors in nuclear energy, who put profits above human lives. And I observed how my fellow activists derided those members of the corporate establishment as image-oriented clones, defined by their identical three-piece suits.

Initially, I felt privileged to be in the company of such idealists. But I soon noticed everyone there was wearing a flannel shirt, jeans, and a down vest. Apparently, the no-nukes movement had its own "three-piece suit." And as the meeting progressed, I sensed that many were participating less out of conviction than to be cool — making them as superficial and homogeneous as their enemies on Wall Street.

During this time, I was also working for an anti-hunger organization. Here, I felt, were genuinely caring individuals with a true calling. Yet their concern for starving children in Biafra didn't extend to people closer to home. The most glaring example was the director herself, the mother of a juvenile delinquent, who was having an affair with her neighbor's husband. Her social values were admirable, but her private life and morals were a disaster.

So maybe there were pitfalls in seeking identity through a cause. But they really showed up once I started exploring Judaism. Even before my first class, I got into a heated discussion with another student about the necessity of religion.

"You don't need religion to give your life meaning," I argued. "For instance, I'm a vegetarian. I get a lot of meaning out of that."

My opponent shot back: "So you're going to worship a carrot?"

Cute, I thought. But her point hit home. Vegetarianism addressed my relationship with animals, the earth, and the world's starving masses, but not my relationship with the people in my own life — or God.

Causes can add meaning to your life, but they can't *be* its meaning. They can define a valuable, healthy part of you, but not the whole you. You're more.

CHAPTER FOUR

The Soul of the Matter

It can take work to get past defining yourself by "what I look like," "what I do," and "what I support" (and while we're at it, let's throw in even weaker sources of self-definition, such as "whom I know," "where I've been," "how much money I have," "what music I like," "what brand of cigarettes I smoke," and whatever else you can think of). If you're having trouble weaning yourself from any of these identities, ask yourself: Who would I be if I didn't have them? If I'm a model, who would I be if I gained 50 pounds? If I'm a marathon runner, who would I be if an accident left me a paraplegic? If I'm an environmentalist, who would I be if corporations decided to be earth-friendly?

The only thing you could be is something that can never be lost, be taken away, or disappear — something eternally yours. This is your core. Judaism calls it your soul. It is nothing less than a spark of God. In his book *Innerspace* (pp. 49-51), Rabbi Aryeh Kaplan explains that in Kabbalistic thought, God is called "nothingness," for God is totally beyond our conception and cannot be defined or characterized. The Hebrew word for "nothingness" is *ain* (*alef-yud-nun*). When rearranged, the letters of *ain* spell the word *ani* (*alef-nun-yud*), "I." This linguistic relationship implies that the real "me" is the "nothingness" within me, the Godly image with which I was created — my soul.

Your soul comprises your deepest thoughts and feelings, those centering on drawing closer to God by becoming a better human being. The true measure of your worth is not how attractive, accomplished, or even devoted to causes you are, but how *good* you are. If your life changes, you may have to find new avenues of self-expression, but that essential self will always exist.

Your soul is what you want to blossom and shine. Ironically, however, you don't accomplish that by highlighting it. Telling everyone how you spent the whole day caring for a sick neighbor calls into question the very spiritual quality of your actions. Spirituality is deep and personal. The less you advertise it, the stronger and more visible it becomes. If you climb a podium and shout into a loudspeaker, "Hey, everyone — listen to how spiritual I am!" you obviously aren't.

When you put your spirituality on display, you lose it — but there is a way to gain it back.

CHAPTER FIVE

Making Your Inner Self Real

Your soul is your essence. You have a body, abilities, and causes, but you don't *have* a soul — you *are* a soul. Judaism teaches you how to reflect it, using everything you have to be everything you are.

The Great Cover-Up

Judaism encourages you to look good — but without flaunting yourself. It urges you to downplay your body in order to reveal your soul. This doesn't mean wearing shapeless, drab clothing. It means being attractive in a way that draws attention past your physicality to your personhood. As a friend puts it, does the way you look scream, "Look what a gorgeous thing I am!"? Or does it whisper, "Now here is an interesting person"?

Religious Jews therefore wear high necklines and relatively long sleeves. Men wear long pants, and women longish skirts. Both sexes avoid tight or flashy clothes. Even in single-sex situations (such as an all-women's gym) or with family, where these rules don't apply, people refrain from uncovering more than what they feel is necessary. (See "Toward the Light of Eden," in chapter 8, for the role of the body in marriage.) Whatever their environment, they cultivate an appearance that demonstrates internal consciousness and self-worth.

By asking us to cover more of our bodies than society demands, Judaism is saying that spirituality shouldn't be reserved for the odd occasion. Whether we're working, shopping, studying, or socializing, internal self-definition is crucial, for it is in our daily lives that our self-image is formed.

Unfortunately, religious dress can be a superficial stand-in for genuine religiosity. Likewise, style can substitute for substance. Both phenomenon are regrettable. Dress is meant to *reflect* your identity, not *replace* it.

The injunction to cover up may smack of a big no-no these days: inhibition. Some fear that educating children to dress modestly may leave them feeling altogether ashamed of their bodies. I've found, however, that if you talk to a child the right way, it isn't hard to inculcate a healthy attitude.

One day, I visited the home of a good friend at her children's bath time. Unbeknownst to her, her freshly washed preschooler had taken a perch on the kitchen windowsill, where he was quite uninhibitedly sunning himself.

"Hey, Dovi," I greeted him with a smile, "you have a

beautiful little bottom there, but don't you think you should put something on it?"

He looked at me innocently. "If it's beautiful — why?"

"Because, Dovi," I explained, "when you cover it, it's easier for me to see your *neshama* [soul]. That's the most beautiful part of you."

The message was heard — with no damage to body image.

Practically speaking, how do you get past your body and focus on your soul?

First of all, work on developing a "soul perspective." As you walk down the street, sit in your office, or interact with others, remind yourself who you really are. And before wearing a particular article of clothing, ask yourself, "Does this detract from or enhance who I am inside?"

Changing your consciousness is just a start, however. There's a Judaic premise that actions affect feelings. (This phenomenon was discussed from a different angle in "Reflected Images," in chapter 1.) With the right intentions — and sometimes even without them — we can change ourselves from the outside in.

The story is told of an evil man who wanted to marry a beautiful woman. But this woman was very good and wanted to marry only someone righteous. So the man put on a righteous- looking mask and acted the part. The woman was fooled and married him. After the wedding, the man continued his charade. Years later, someone who knew how evil this man was heard how he had tricked this poor woman and wanted her to know the truth. He went to their home and ripped off the man's disguise. To his amazement, the face beneath it was identical to the mask! After years of acting righteously, the evil man had actually become good. The outside had affected the inside.

So if you want to become more inner-oriented, start dressing the part. Wear less revealing and looser-fitting clothing. Keep your hair neat. Button up an extra button. Be attractive, not attract*ing*.

As a friend describes it, personal growth is like building muscle. You have to exercise just beyond your comfort level. If you do less, you won't get anywhere. If you do more, you may injure yourself. So too with covering up. Work up to it. Accept occasional regressions as part of the process. But stick to it, and little by little, you'll notice the subtle (or not so subtle) difference in how others relate to you — and how you relate to yourself.

Moving Your Center Offstage

Just as Judaism wants you to look good in a way that reflects your soul, it encourages you to develop your God-given abilities — but without spotlighting them. Defining yourself internally means being secure enough not to need others' attention or validation. Judaism therefore urges you not to make your talents, skills, and accomplishments your identity, but to integrate them into the deeper picture of who you are.

Contrary to what some may think (and as Jan discovered, in chapter 2), lowering your profile won't cost you socially — if you're looking to meet quality people, that is. For a quality person is drawn to someone whose sense of self lies within. Rabbi Akiba, the great 2nd century sage, was an illiterate shepherd when noticed by Rachel, who defied her wealthy father and married him. Rachel's greatness — her vision of his potential, her steadfast encouragement, and her willingness to sacrifice tremendously for his growth — allowed him to become a brilliant Torah scholar and leader of the Jewish people. The Talmud (*Ketubot* 62b) recounts that Rachel was drawn to him because of the quiet internality he radiated.

Unlike necklines and sleeve lengths, internal self-definition in "doing" isn't always clear-cut. At one extreme, some behaviors are beyond the pale. (I recall an old acquaintance, "Wrong Way" Wooten, who would bicycle through town sitting backwards on his handlebars, warbling "The Girl's All Right with Me" over an amplifier. Entertaining guy, but he apparently hadn't heard about internality.) At the other extreme, burying your talents or abilities forever would be a shame if they might enrich your own and others' lives. The challenge is to find a healthy place between these two poles, and then, focusing not on what you do but on how you do it, make it clear that your identity lies far beneath your "performance."

Many years ago, I asked my rabbi if it was appropriate for me to address male-female audiences in *kiruv* (outreach) programs, knowing that some religious women won't.

"It depends on your presence," he told me. "Putting on a show wouldn't be appropriate. But if you're imparting ideas that will benefit others, and doing so with dignity, there's no problem." In other words, internal consciousness exists when you emphasize not form but content — not your image but your message.

In addition to lecturers, I know musicians, actors, dancers, and even a mime who maintain their center beautifully. They probably don't even think of themselves as "performers." Rather, they use their gifts simply as vehicles for sharing something of meaning or beauty (or just fun or humor) with their audiences.

As mentioned, it is men who more often fall for selling themselves by "what I do." A deep-thinking male will escape this trap, knowing that the only truly worthwhile accomplishments involve not "what I do" but "who I am" — and that a truly worthwhile female knows this as well. As another college classmate recently put it: "I've learned that I'm not the title on my business card. Kindness, generosity of spirit, and integrity are the real cargo to hold on to."

If you don't want to define yourself by what you do, once again, continually remind yourself that you a soul, and embrace the "actions lead to feelings" principle. Avoid the limelight. Make space for others. Resist the impulse to impress them. Let yourself be appreciated not for your accomplishments, but for your qualities — and begin feeling centered within yourself.

Bringing the Revolution Home

Judaism encourages your participation in worthy causes — but not as a banner for your identity. Instead, they should be part of your essential commitment to goodness.

A college classmate who has made careers out of his causes tells his students: "Never aspire to public office; aspire to public service." In other words, focus not on your own image or importance, but on others' needs.

Most important, Judaism wants us to be consistent. The desire to help society is healthiest when noble social ideals are grounded in personal morality, and when every human's worth is manifest in your own relationships. If you're a genuine idealist, your first "cause" must be self-transformation, for true, enduring goodness starts inside. To fix the world, you must first fix yourself.

If you don't want your causes to define you, make sure that you're involved in them for the right reasons, and that they reflect how you live the rest of your life. Rather than attaching yourself to popular, "cool" causes, volunteer for things like driving elderly people to their doctors' appointments. Make your contributions behind the scenes, where image is less a factor. If motherhood claims all your time and energy, realize that running a shelter for unwanted children is no more valuable than the far less glamorous job of caring for your own. Finally, as Alan Morinis (*Climbing Jacob's Ladder*, pp. 152-153) quotes Rabbi Yechiel Yitzchok Perr as saying: Don't substitute reaching out for reaching in. Regard your involvement in causes, in Morinis's words, not just as working *for* others, but as working *on* yourself. Focus on improving your character — and reap the rewards of true personal growth.

The Spirit Within

Judaism encourages you to develop spiritually — but privately. The Jew stands not before an audience but before God, who measures greatness not by others' admiration, but by righteousness. Isaac allowing himself to be brought as a sacrifice (Genesis 22), Joseph forgiving his brothers for having sold him into slavery (Genesis 45), Boaz allowing Ruth to sleep at his feet all night without touching her (Ruth 3) — these extraordinary individuals neither sought nor won public acclaim, for their triumphs took place on the inner stage.

Furthermore, according to Jewish tradition, the world is maintained in every generation through the merit of 36 especially righteous individuals. Yet no one knows who they are, for their righteousness is hidden.

Judaism likewise praises us when we perform *mitzvot* in a hidden way. For example, *tzedaka* is best given anonymously, not for applause but for its own sake. When you refrain from drawing attention to your good deeds or character, you strengthen your spiritual core — the part of you that knows God is the only One whose approval matters.

Herein lies the difference between false spirituality and the real thing:

A pseudo-spiritualist seeks attention more for himself than for his message. He may make public appearances in which he lauds his piety, even proclaiming himself (explicitly or implicitly) a savior. While his charisma may attract a large following, his "spirituality" is nothing but an ego trip.

The possessor of genuine spirituality has no desire to parade it. Great rabbis of previous generations shied away from publicity, fearing it would devalue their deeds (see *Michtav Me'Eliyahu*, p. 60). Jewish leaders become such not by promoting themselves but by *being* themselves. Despite this humility — or because of it — people see who they are and flock to them.

The mark of spiritual greatness is internality.

If you want your soul to shine, don't broadcast it. Do a good deed and don't tell anyone. Perform not only visible *mitzvot* but those no one can see, such as working on conquering a negative character trait, studying Torah privately, or praying alone. And know that God is smiling.

Tzniut

The internal self-definition we've been discussing is what Judaism calls *tzniut*. *Tzniut* begins with the consciousness that you are a soul: that your deepest self strives for better relationships with others and with God. It then means expressing that soul by letting your body, achievements, causes, and everything else about you reflect it rather than overshadow it. *Tzniut* comes from the same root as *tzin'a*, "privacy," for it means knowing what to keep private and what to show, and when and how, so you can project and cultivate an internal self-image. *Tzniut* therefore includes thought, speech, and action, for in every realm there is a time to reveal and a time to conceal.

Judaism seeks to instill *tzniut* from a young age. When parents call their little boy not "adorable," "superstar," or "our little activist," but "*neshama'le*" ("little soul"), his face shines. When a little girl is praised for her *middot* (character traits), her face registers something deeper than pride. Raised on *tzniut*, these "little souls" reach adulthood with their unconscious self-perceptions anchored in qualities they intuitively know to be deep and real.

We are often impressed by sophistication, status, image. Yet *tzniut*, at its highest level, results in a profound, image-free way of being. Underlying it may be tremendous complexity — or, just as powerfully, simplicity.

Perhaps one of the best expressions of *tzniut* I've heard came from a religious man whom a very worldly, accomplished friend of mine was dating. "What are your dreams, your ambitions, your aspirations?" she wanted to know.

He replied simply, "To do good."

CHAPTER SIX

The Feminine Connection

While *tzniut* is essential for both sexes, it is emphasized for females. The Midrash (Genesis *Rabba* 18:2) recounts that God created woman from the rib, an internal part of the body, while pronouncing upon each of her limbs: "Be a woman who embodies *tzniut*."

The different dress codes for Orthodox men and women reflect this emphasis. Men dress according to community sensitivities. Where *tzniut* is taken seriously, males dress as modestly as females (albeit in their own way). Yet women adhere to an absolute standard wherever they live.

A further difference can be seen in "who's wearing the pants." Pants outline and emphasize private parts of the body more than a loose-fitting skirt. Originally, therefore, neither Jewish women nor Jewish men wore pants without a dress or tunic over them. With time, most men drifted away from this level of *tzniut*, while religious women have by and large upheld it.

Observant women likewise avoid attracting male attention. On festive occasions, for example, the sexes usually dance on separate sides of a partition. It's much easier for women to be themselves (and have fun) when they aren't concerned about how men are looking at them.

Women and *Tzniut*

The emphasis on *tzniut* for females can be appreciated in the light of practical realities. Men usually attribute tremendous importance to a woman's appearance. Women, on the other hand, while not oblivious to a man's looks, are typically more interested in his love (or something that feels like it). Consequently, women often attempt to win that love by playing (consciously or semiconsciously) to men's regard for externals.

This strategy can spell disaster for a woman. Most tragically, one accustomed to "getting" a man this way will internalize an increasingly shallow self-image, losing sight of what she has to offer. Furthermore, while her feelings for this man may deepen, his may not. I know a woman who believed her boyfriend of several months loved her. She was rudely awakened upon discovering that his feelings for her were no deeper than when she first attracted his attention at the local pizza shop.

Since a woman is at greater risk of equating her self-worth with her outside — and winning a very questionable "love" — it pays for her to protect herself through *tzniut*.

Aside from this practical argument, *tzniut* is more intrinsic to women.

Judaism understands that God created the physical world as a vehicle for spirituality. Good food, fine wine, a beautiful home, art, music, the outdoors — all can bring us closer to God. So can our bodies.

A woman's physicality encompasses more than a man's. Pregnancy, childbirth, and lactation are all profound experiences of her womanhood. In addition, more of her body is potentially arousing (as is obvious from advertising). Her consequent power to attract and influence men is well known to both sexes — and can either destroy her deeper self or express it. Parallel to this stronger sensual dimension and presence, women are gifted with a greater propensity for *tzniut* — the sensitivity of knowing when to conceal and when to reveal.

Yet the physical world is not only a vehicle for spirituality but a reflection of deeper spiritual reality. That the organs defining a female are inside (whereas a male's are largely outside) teaches us about female souls: A woman's spiritual expression, more than a man's, is meant to be internal and private. Psalms (45:15) affirms this in a famous and beautiful statement: "All the glory of the king's daughter is within."

While some people feel the degree of *tzniut* observed by religious women is sufficient, others apparently think we could do better. "If you don't want to be superficially defined," a young woman once challenged me, "why don't you go all the way and wear a long-sleeved, floor-length, shapeless, dark-colored dress and a veil, like Muslim women?"

Having never been a practicing Muslim, I can't explain that "uniform." Its practical effect, however, is to shroud women and make them more or less identical. This loss of presence and individuality is antithetical to Judaism. The Jewish concept of *tzniut* aims not to negate a woman's physical self but to use it to express her true identity. Jewish women's faces are visible, as the face (in Hebrew, "*panim*") reflects a person's inside ("*penim*"). While downplaying their sensuality, Jewish women are to be well-dressed, feminine, and even quietly distinctive. *Tzniut* therefore requires sensitivity, as there's a fine line between attractive and attracting. But Judaism knows women can meet this challenge.

After considering how to look good, a woman must consider where. While it's tempting to dress up to go out, the Jewish ideal is to dress up (albeit comfortably) to stay *in*. Looking your best in your own living room is a beautiful way to show your spouse you love him. (This goes for husbands, too.) In fact, the Midrash (*Tanchuma*, "*VaYishlach*" 5) notes that jewelry was given to women so they might adorn themselves not in public but at home.

Since a Jewish woman doesn't hide behind a shapeless dress or a veil, some man may find her distracting. Judaism tells him: "She's doing her part. Now it's your turn. If you can't look at her appropriately, don't look." (This goes for women looking at men, too.)

Keep It Under Your Hat

The most distinguishing feature of religious Jewish female dress is the head covering a married woman wears. Be it a hat, beret, scarf, snood, turban, wig, fall, or creative combination of any of the above, she'll have something on her head, and her hair will be under it.

Religious single women anticipate this practice with a wide range of feelings. One who's really into her hair may recoil at the idea of covering it (though that may be exactly what she needs to pull her self-image inward). Those who dread "bad hair days" are relieved to kiss them goodbye. Others are unenthusiastic but determined to make the best of it: "If I have to cover my hair, I'm going to have fun doing it!" And some greet the whole issue with nothing more than a shrug.

Of course, any person's feelings about this aspect of *tzniut* will be colored by what she sees as the reason. A popular idea is that since a woman's hair is attractive (how many models are bald?), she should "save it for her husband." Certainly, when a woman's hair is covered in public, it enhances the intimate bond with her husband when revealed to him. Yet this rationale overlooks the fact that divorcées and widows also cover their hair.

Hair covering, while commonly considered part of *tzniut*, is actually its own mitzvah. At least two explanations can be offered, both reflecting a profound and irreversible change a woman undergoes upon marrying.

One significant passage traditionally associated with marriage is from naïveté to direct knowledge of intimacy between husband and wife. While deeply transforming for both sexes, Judaism understands this event to impact most upon a female. It opens her eyes not only to a profound dimension of her womanhood but to its power. As a result, she's more tuned in and responsive to male-female chemistry. And when such a woman displays something sensual of herself, it radiates more "energy" than in the past, because of her experiential new awareness of what it can evoke.

Hair is sensual. Young women in particular can often be seen brushing it from their eyes, combing their fingers through it, sweeping it off their foreheads so it immediately falls back, putting it loosely in a ponytail and seconds later letting it cascade down — most conspicuously when guys are around. Though their hair is apparently so in the way, few women wear it in a bun. They know (as do men) that hair has a special appeal.

When a woman covers her hair after marriage, she makes an important statement, first and foremost to herself: "I now understand the power of my sensuality — and I intend to keep it between my husband and me." (According to one Jewish legal opinion, even an unmarried woman who's no longer innocent should cover her hair, although this isn't done.) As a newlywed friend described it: "Covering my hair made me rethink who I am. My look became more adult and lost its flirtatiousness. I knew how strong my appeal could be, and I wanted to channel it toward only one man."

Yet marriage brings about other changes as well: It opens

the door to new levels of self- and other-awareness, opportunities for emulating God through profound, multifaceted giving, and for achieving the wholeness that exists only in the union of male and female. Entering this new world is a significant "coming of age" that confers upon a person a higher standing in the eyes of the community.

Judaism, along with many contemporary psychologists and feminists, sees women as defining themselves largely through relationships. After all, Adam was created alone, whereas Eve was created as a partner. Thus, more than a man, a woman "comes into her own" in marriage, so her status changes more markedly. In a society that exalts independence, all this may offend. To the Jewish mind, however, life is about relationships, of which — next to our relationship with God — marriage is the ultimate.

Cross-culturally and historically, when we want recognition of our status, we draw attention to our heads. A student graduating university wears a distinctive, tasseled, four-cornered cap. Religious dignitaries wear impressive headgear. The chief of a Native American tribe wears the largest headdress. All intuitively understand that the head, the mind, is the seat of our humanness, and by emphasizing it, we emphasize our human stature.

From this perspective, a married woman covers her head as a sign — both to others and herself — of her greater dignity. (Accordingly, even a bald woman would cover her head.) Someone I know who wears beautiful head coverings once overheard two non-Jewish women commenting on how regal she looked. Many women, in fact, regard their head covering as a queen does her crown.

While a married woman can revert to being single, she cannot reverse either her sexual or her spiritual awakening, and therefore divorced and widowed women generally continue covering their hair. Here, however, exceptions can be made, in which case the perceived reason for hair/head covering will be a deciding factor.

A woman I know who was married only briefly before divorcing questioned whether she should continue covering her head, fearing her appearance might make it harder to get a job or remarry. Lacking evidence that either would be the case, her rabbi invoked the "stature principle." "Ask your friends how they view you," he suggested. "Do they look up to you more because you were married, or do they see you just as you were before?"

Religious men, too, observe customs that associate head covering with marriage. In many circles, men begin wearing hats more consistently upon marrying. Most Ashkenazi men start praying with a tallit, and while Sephardim do so from their bar mitzvah or even earlier, most wear it over their heads only once married.

Whichever approach a woman prefers, the ideas of reserving her sexuality and expressing her dignity are intertwined. Just as "letting your hair down" connotes both sensual self-display and less dignity, covering the hair and thus toning down one's sensuality goes hand in hand with increased respect as a married woman.

Many people don't understand why some religious authorities permit women to wear wigs. "Isn't is hypocritical," they contest, "to cover your head with something that looks like your own hair — or even better?"

Some wigs reflect the spirit of the law, helping a woman look put-together yet non-provocative and dignified. And just as she may improve her appearance with makeup or a girdle, she may wear a wig that's nicer than her hair.

On the other hand, a wig that draws attention to itself rather than to the personhood of the wearer — because it's conspicuously large, long, shiny, unusually styled or colored, or outright seductive — is not what any rabbi had in mind. So too for wigs designed to make a woman look as if she weren't wearing one. Just as it's fallacious to believe, "It doesn't matter how I dress, because I know who I am" (see "Reflected Images," in chapter 2), it's equally mistaken to think, "It doesn't matter if people think it's my hair, because I know I'm covering it." A woman who looks single will have trouble feeling married and developing her self-image accordingly.

A female can and should look good. After the wedding, her challenge is how to do so in a way that commands respect for her as a married woman — both in others' eyes and in her own.

Strengthening the Weaker Sex

I've stressed that the fundamental purpose of *tzniut* is to create and preserve an internal self-image. Yet there's a secondary aspect, specific to women: assuming partial responsibility for the effect of one's attire upon men. Males are easily distracted by provocatively dressed females. Once distracted, it's their choice whether to continue being distracted, but that initial look is a knee-jerk reaction, and what follows usually isn't conducive to spiritual growth.

I know a young woman who started dressing more modestly for this reason. Though not observant, she appreciated that the religious, male high school students she passed every day were being taught to respect women, and she understood how scantily clad females could undermine this education. Guessing these guys already faced enough challenges, she chose not to pose another.

Many women, however, don't acknowledge their effect upon men. A newly religious, single guy told me: "I think most women are in denial about how their dress affects us. They see themselves as good people who just happen to wear very little. When such a woman helps an old lady carry her bags, she may feel great, thinking, 'Look how I've impacted this person's life.' But she's making a bigger — and far different — impact on every guy who sees her."

Most significantly, many guys whose heads are turned by provocatively dressed women are other women's husbands. Most would prefer not to think about anyone other than their wives — and their wives would concur. Men who don't feel this way need feminine distraction even less.

And then there are the wives. No married woman benefits from being rated against "better" bodies on the street.

Neither, for that matter, do single women. As author Marina Goodman puts it: "A woman who argues that 'men should deal with their own problem' and therefore wears whatever she wants doesn't realize she may be hurting other women. For me, *tzniut* is an expression of sisterhood."

This focus on others comes to the fore in the realm of *kol isha*, the "(singing) voice of a woman."

Music touches the soul. Indeed, Jews have always embraced singing as a vehicle for spiritual elevation. Yet Judaism understands that a woman's singing — like revealing clothing — can arouse men. Witness the appeal of popular female singers. (Even the ancient Greeks enshrined *kol isha* in the myth of the Sirens, whose beautiful voices singing from the cliffs above the ocean would lure sailors to crash their ships on the rocks.)

Furthermore, singing can be a subtle yet powerful self-revelation. Its emotion can expose one's deepest self. (Instrumental music alone has something of this effect. A newly observant friend, who sensed the "vibes" her beautiful guitar playing created on a date, later asked me, "Are you sure I was allowed to do that?")

Thus, a woman's voice is doubly attractive, coupling attraction with a feeling of intimacy, much as touch does. (See my book *The Magic Touch*.)

Interestingly, Judaism feels not that a woman compromises her spirituality by singing in front of men, but that men are compromised by listening. Men are therefore prohibited from hearing women (other than close relatives) sing; and only as a consequence, women don't sing in front of men. In other words, females refrain from *kol isha* purely for men's sake.

This restraint is certainly lofty — but not necessarily easy.

A woman who's unhappy observing *kol isha* can respond in numerous ways. One is to stew in resentment (as I initially did). A more productive solution is to adopt valid leniencies within Jewish law whenever possible (such as that permitting group singing of Shabbat songs).

Another option is to see *kol isha* as promoting an essential Jewish trait: other-orientedness. This means putting yourself aside — temporarily, in a healthy, giving way — for another's good. Other-orientedness is a foundation of the Jewish way of life.

Whatever response a woman chooses, she'll hopefully have other opportunities to sing. "For women, by women" performances provide a deeply satisfying outlet for musical creativity as well as fostering wonderful energy, joy, and sisterhood.

Even if men are present, they can often be sensitized to women's love of singing. When my husband is the only adult male at our Shabbat table, he often excuses himself early to let our female guests sing. Most religious men have no desire to stifle others and, once asked, can be quite accommodating.

Kol isha offers a unique challenge in the realm of *tzniut*. Yet the woman who observes it receives unique spiritual dividends — by caring for others.

Love Insurance

Female *tzniut* is particularly influential in marriage.

The Talmud (*Yevamot* 62b) states: "Any man without a wife lives without a protective wall." Marriage "protects" a man from himself by providing a holy outlet for his sexual needs. Yet having a wife doesn't necessarily prevent him from seeing who else is available. Some wives have therefore gone on the offensive, attempting to out-entice every other female on the street. This tactic is not only degrading but self-defeating, however, since aging will eventually put them out of the competition.

Better a woman should enhance her husband's appreciation of the unique benefits of marriage. By embracing *tzniut* in consciousness and action, she encourages him to develop a deeper, multifaceted relationship with her that will underlie and empower their physical bond, making it like none other he could have. At the same time, she creates an aura of privacy, intensity, and specialness around physical intimacy, which keeps it compelling.

While a man is responsible for his own behavior, his wife can help protect him from doing what he shouldn't — by eliminating his desire to.

Womanpower

As Tziporah Heller notes in *More Precious than Pearls* (pp. 40-44), *tzniut* has given Jewish women tremendous spiritual strength. For the more a woman recognizes her inner value, the less she'll care what others think of her. Rather than being pulled by whatever she hears, she'll be able to heed a higher calling. And the more her sense of self transcends appearances, the deeper her vision of the world. With this perception, external obstacles are less overwhelming and problems more surmountable.

Such was the power of Sarah Schneirer, the great educator who single-handedly revolutionized Torah study for women. In her last lesson before her death (as recounted in *Carry Me in Your Heart* by Pearl Benisch, p. 321), she told her students: "A Jewish woman must always carry a note in each pocket — one saying, 'All the glory of the king's daughter is within,' and the other saying, 'It is time to act for God.'" Sarah Schneirer was a model of *tzniut* and at the same time an activist. For *tzniut* need not silence us. On the contrary, defining ourselves internally should help us find our true voice and the courage to speak out.

Jewish women have often faced great challenges — not least to resist society's definitions of self and create their own. *Tzniut* is a wellspring of support in helping women, and through them the rest of the world, become everything they can be. Perhaps this is why the Sages tell us (Ruth *Rabba* 4:4) that "each generation is redeemed by its righteous women."

CHAPTER SEVEN

The Transformation

T*zniut* means drawing all aspects of yourself inward and letting them emanate from your soul. It gradually transforms you into a person whose quiet, centered energy says: "I know who I am and what I have to give — and when."

This internal self-definition frees you from society's fluctuating assessments of desirability. For example, in the 1920s Miss America contestants were pleasantly plump; today they're anorexic. Who knows what kind of body will be in vogue in the future, and the consequence for millions of women's self-esteem? *Tzniut* helps us transcend trends and root ourselves in eternal values.

But *tzniut* is even more empowering. Through the strength of their souls, individuals brought light even into Auschwitz. Viktor Frankl, in his famous treatise *Man's Search for Meaning*, writes (pp. 104-106):

> We who lived in concentration camps can remember the men who walked through the huts comforting

> others, giving away their last piece of bread. They may have been few in number, but they offer sufficient proof that everything can be taken from a man but one thing: the last of human freedoms — to choose one's attitude in any given set of circumstances, to choose one's own way. ... It is this spiritual freedom — which cannot be taken away — that makes life meaningful and purposeful.

Your looks may fade, along with your accomplishments and causes, but your soul is always there. This is what *tzniut* reminds us.

Getting the "Look"

Tzniut doesn't mean blending into the wallpaper. On the contrary, its magnetism is subtle yet unmistakable. Many years ago I attended a function at which I found myself in the company of a very religious, native Jerusalemite. She was exceptionally attractive: Her slim figure was clothed in a modest yet becoming dress, and the azure scarf covering her hair accentuated her fine features and clear, glowing complexion. But as I gazed at her, I was drawn to her inner beauty. She had a power — very different from other women's, and far more compelling.

Unfortunately, not all religious people pull this off.

"What about the girl I just saw?" a non-observant young man once confronted me. "Her shirt had a high enough neckline and three-quarter-length sleeves, but it was skin-tight and barely covered her stomach. And though her skirt was past her knees, it had a slit and clung to her bottom. I wouldn't call that 'internality' — I'd call it the 'religious provocative look.'"

Sadly, that girl hadn't absorbed that beauty is more than skin-deep.

One day my daughter came out of her room wearing a friend's skirt, which fit her quite snugly. I looked at her and took a deep breath. "Sweetheart," I began, "I know you love that skirt and want to wear it so much, but I don't think you can."

"Why not?" she demanded. "It's long enough!"

"Yes, but the second I saw you, my eyes automatically went to your bottom. And I think you want to be seen as more than that."

With a sigh, she returned to her room, reappearing a few minutes later in something her size.

"Ahh," I said, smiling. "Now you look beautiful, inside and out."

She beamed.

Skirt length can be measured; *tzniut* cannot. Anyone can play by the "rules" of *tzniut* but thwart their intention, for the "rules" work only when one identifies with their objective. The problem, according to Tziporah Heller, is that we breathe in superficiality like air, then can't disassociate from what we've become. *Tzniut* means rejecting society's standards and defining "looking good" in a deeper way.

Reclaiming Our Bodies

One symptom of defining ourselves by our bodies is obsession with weight. Western culture idolizes thinness — particularly for women. Every spring, ladies frantically undertake to lose those extra pounds accumulated during the winter, so they can survive the upcoming "swimsuit competition." At the opposite extreme, several women I know have attributed overeating to an unconscious resistance to being objectified. In either case, women's weight — and the eating disorders that plague the Western world — is dictated by outside forces.

When women adopt *tzniut*, interesting things happen. A "complier" — who has struggled to be thin in order to please men — often puts on some healthy pounds. While she may initially go overboard, she usually comes around to her desirable weight, but because she wants it for *herself*. A "rejectionist" — who has gained weight in order *not* to please men — often finds she can now be slim while still being a person. Some women drop both their excess pounds and their unhealthy relationship with food after developing a more internal way of thinking and dressing.

In either case — and whether you're male or female — if you want control over your body, your weight must be dictated only by self-respect (and health). And *tzniut* goes a long way toward building it.

Making a Difference

Some people, upon starting to dress and act with *tzniut*,

feel disempowered by no longer commanding superficial attention. But one's power should never come from another's less spiritual side. Power is the ability to effect change — be it raising someone's hormone levels or, preferably, moving people toward spirituality.

The biblical book of Esther, read on Purim, describes how Esther, after being taken into King Ahasuerus's palace, obeyed Mordechai's command not to reveal her nationality. For nine years, she didn't talk about herself. Nonetheless, the Midrash (*Otzar HaMidrashim*, p. 60) tells us, she so inspired her maidservants that when she revealed she was Jewish, they all converted to Judaism. The Talmud (*Megilla* 13b) cites Esther's silence as an outstanding example of *tzniut*. At the same time, when she did speak, her words came from her deepest self and touched the deepest selves of others.

In encouraging us to influence others with our souls, *tzniut* catalyzes social change. Every movement toward internal self-definition creates a ripple effect. In asking others to seek the real you, you challenge them to define the real them. The more people who arrive at the right answer, the healthier our society. In Rabbi Aryeh Kaplan's words (*Innerspace*, p. 51), when you connect your will to God's will, your potential for transforming the world is unlimited. *Tzniut* creates that connection.

Nurturing Nature

While our bodies can overshadow our inner selves, not

everyone accepts covering up as the solution. "If you ask me," an innovator will propose, "we should all wear *less*, or even *nothing*. If we just got used to seeing people's bodies, we could get past them."

This suggestion (usually offered by someone who hates to shop) is naïve. No matter how accustomed we might become to unclothed bodies, their sheer physicality would still be in our face, distracting us from the essential man or woman inside.

It's true, however, that if the innovator had his way, the body would no longer arouse. But that would be a shame. For if the sight of the opposite sex doesn't move us, we've lost something precious.

In her book *A Return to Modesty* (p. 53), Wendy Shalit cites research that men shown pictures of barely clothed models later described themselves as less in love with their wives. Visual overkill creates superficial comparisons and destroys specialness. How sad — and avoidable. Rather than desensitizing ourselves, *tzniut* asks us to *re*-sensitize.

I once listened as a young man tried to convey this concept to his father, who didn't understand why his newly religious son would go only to a men's-only beach. "Isn't this a bit much?" his father wanted to know. "After all, everyone goes to 'mixed' beaches. Only you religious people think it's a big deal."

"But Dad," his son countered, "that's exactly it. When a man sees a woman wearing practically nothing, it *should* be a 'big deal' — and it *would* be, if the only woman he saw like that were his wife!"

Dad's wife sat quietly, presenting a united parental front. But she was listening intently.

"Maybe you have a point," his father admitted. "But it means you'll have to pass up some great vacation spots. Isn't that a high price to pay?"

"It depends what's more important," the son replied. "I may miss out on a few beaches, but I'll really appreciate the beauty of a woman's body — and once I'm married, both my wife and I will benefit. She'll be that much more special to me."

"Well, that sounds nice, but I don't know how practical it is," his father answered. "And as for me, I'm not sure it's worth it."

His wife glared at him, as if to say, "It's not?!"

You undoubtedly crave specialness with your spouse. And like many things in life, you may have to give up something to get it. But it *is* worth it. When sexual attraction is confined to marriage, it's intensified — which may be one of the best fringe benefits of covering up.

Young and Old

Although *tzniut* is best internalized when introduced in childhood, we can assimilate it later in life.

I know a woman named Shari who prefers the "natural look" over makeup. One day, while visiting her friend Debbie, the latter took out her cosmetic case.

"My husband's coming home soon," she explained, "and he appreciates when I look my best."

"Doesn't it bother you," Shari sputtered, "that what your husband appreciates isn't your real face?"

"No," Debbie responded calmly. "He knows I'm wearing makeup. But what if he didn't? What if he lived his whole life thinking this is how I really look? Would it matter?"

"Of course!" Shari exclaimed. "Don't you want to be loved for who you are?"

"With or without makeup," Debbie said gently, "my looks are not who I am."

Suddenly Shari realized that in taking an ideological stance on makeup, it was she who defined herself by her looks.

Another person I know had a similar awakening when her face was badly burned, and cosmetic surgery couldn't restore its original appearance. Confronting a different "me" in the mirror drove home where her true self lay.

Physical limitations can have the same effect. When a professional harpist I know broke her wrist and couldn't play for months, she realized her identity must be deeper. Another woman, her career in finance cut short by chronic illness, described how her life changed as a result: "These past years have taught me more than all my years in university or investment banking. I've had time to read and think, to grow spiritually and religiously. I've become involved with a group of high-risk children, and I've joined the boards of several non-profit organizations. None of this would have happened had I not succumbed to a disabling disease."

Aging affords us all the opportunity to plumb our deeper

selves. Instead of doing that, however, many of us panic. A man approaching 50 will have a midlife crisis, divorce his wife of 25 years, and marry someone his daughter's age in a desperate attempt to regain his youth. A woman will color her hair, endure face-lift after face-lift, and starve herself into svelteness. Neither understands that aging is a blessing in disguise, preparing us for the next life — which Judaism calls the world of truth — in which we'll be all soul. With this perspective, we can always possess inner beauty, no matter how gray and wrinkled we become. As someone once said: "You can take no credit for beauty at sixteen. But if you are beautiful at sixty, it will be your soul's own doing." In drawing our self-definition inward, aging puts us back in touch with ourselves. A man in his mid-40s observed, "Perhaps one reason people tend to become more comfortable with themselves as they age is that they are actually re-becoming themselves."

Young or old, the key to happiness is knowing who we are.

One morning, I entered my children's bedroom to find my five-year-old daughter lying dreamily in her bed. Upon seeing me, she smiled a lovely, sweet, "good morning" smile.

I smiled back. "You look especially pretty this morning," I told her. "Do you know why?"

A beautiful light filled her eyes as she answered softly, "My *neshama*."

CHAPTER EIGHT

Is There a Chance for Love?

As great as the ramifications of *tzniut* are upon the individual, they extend much further, embracing all our relationships, even with God.

Preoccupation with Others

Tzniut fosters true *chessed*, lovingkindness.

Chessed flourishes when those performing it aren't wondering how they look or what others think of them, but are focused solely on those to whom they are giving. For this reason, the Talmud (*Sukka* 49b) gives as examples of *tzniut* the *mitzvot* of attending a funeral and rejoicing with a bride. These are clearly acts of kindness, but why *tzniut*? Because rather than being self-conscious, one's attention is totally on the other. When paying one's last respects, one hopefully isn't thinking, "Is my outfit solemn enough?" And when dancing with a bride, few thoughts are more irrelevant than, "Do people think I'm graceful?" While *tzniut* initially requires introspection, it ultimately frees you from self-preoccupation so you can focus outward.

When the biblical Jacob sought to marry Rachel, he correctly suspected that her wily father, Laban, might trick him by substituting her older sister, Leah, under the wedding canopy (Rashi on Genesis 29:2). He therefore taught Rachel secret signs by which he would be able to recognize his veiled bride. But all she could think of was the pain and humiliation Leah would suffer upon being discovered, so Rachel gave her the signs. According to the Talmud (*Megilla* 13b), Rachel's selfless identification with her sister epitomizes *tzniut*.

Ending the Longest War

Tzniut can transform male-female relationships.

Men and women today have many gripes about each other. Women complain that men are "animals" and can't commit to a relationship. Men, on the other hand, complain that women rate them by their worldly achievements and earning power.

Interestingly, I rarely hear such grievances from people who live by Torah values. Why?

It's all about expectations and behavior.

Religious women (taking their cue from the Torah) expect men to view them appropriately, behave decently, and appreciate marriage. And *tzniut* dictates that they dress and act in ways likely to inspire men to meet these expectations.

Sadly, in Western society, women expect the worst of

men, unwittingly (and sometimes wittingly) encourage it, and then complain about it. In fact, men are far from hopeless. They're not animals; they're easily distracted souls. Their outsides seek physical pleasure; their insides crave commitment and love. In approaching them, many women mistakenly work from the outside in. When a woman chooses internality instead, she challenges a man to relate to her more deeply from the start, immediately putting him in touch with his soul — and they both reap the reward.

Men whose lives revolve around Torah also avoid many frustrations of their secular counterparts. A truly religious man expects a woman to value him primarily for his connection to God and his performance of *mitzvot*. Through *tzniut*, he inspires appreciation not for what he does but for who he is.

The *Yale Alumni Magazine* regularly advertises a dating service called "The Right Stuff" — that is, Ivy League graduates. Yet brilliance doesn't make one a better mate. Whom would you rather marry: an inconsiderate academic, or someone simple but caring? And who would you rather be? What's the real "right stuff"?

Character defines a person's worth — and character is rooted in the soul. *Tzniut* encourages us to look past IQ, exterior, and income. It reduces the chances of infatuation — and disillusionment — based on such factors. It reminds you, as I wrote in *Head to Heart*, that you want to marry an essence, not an image.

But it does far more.

Three unfortunate trends (among others) characterize Western society: emphasis on the physical, preoccupation with self, and frustration with the opposite sex. It's no coincidence that these phenomena appeared one after the other and continue to flourish together. For the more we dehumanize others by relating first and foremost to their bodies, the less we care about their feelings and needs. And the more we occupy the center of our universe, the more we reduce others to vehicles for our own gratification. Amid this superficiality and selfishness, relationships fail.

Judaism, in opposition (as usual), teaches that a relationship succeeds when partners value each other and act accordingly. *Tzniut* pulls the rug out from under shallow attraction, replacing it with a foundation of genuine admiration and caring. This attitude leads to giving — the basis of love — and to a strong, spiritual, lifelong relationship.

Moving Close

Tzniut makes genuine intimacy possible.

Someone I know once commented, "No wonder so many people have trouble with intimate relationships when they don't even have one with themselves." Intimacy is sharing, which means knowing what you have to share. King Solomon (Proverbs 11:2) stated 3,000 years ago: "Those who have *tzniut* have wisdom." Among other things, *tzniut* grants us the wisdom to know ourselves, then know what to look for in bonding with others.

Intimacy, however, requires selectivity. Selling yourself

to everyone you meet doesn't leave anyone feeling particularly close to you. Intimacy develops only when you keep enough of yourself private that self-revelation is meaningful. As Wendy Shalit puts it (p. 136), "If nothing is secret, nothing is sacred." When you allow only a few people to find out what makes you unique — and one very special person to unearth it more fully — each will feel a greater appreciation for and connection with the "you" he or she gradually discovers.

Toward the Light of Eden

If internal consciousness is so important to a relationship, why not dress modestly even in times of marital intimacy?

As explained, God created us with the ability to see our outsides and insides as one. Unfortunately, that's not how we see each other today. But there's one realm in which we can regain a piece of that lost world: marriage. If your marriage is rooted in spirituality, your spouse's outer and inner selves merge.

Such was the relationship, the Torah tells us, between Abraham and Sarah. Traveling toward Egypt and fearing that the immoral Egyptians might desire his wife, Abraham told her (Genesis 12:11), "I now realize you are a beautiful woman." Why only "now," after so many years of marriage? Abraham put himself in an Egyptian mindset and saw Sarah as a man devoid of Godliness might see her — as an object. He himself had never viewed her this way.

In a committed, loving marriage, we don't strive to "get past" the body by covering it. Starting from the wedding night, the dissonance between outside and inside gradually turns to harmony. Over the years, physical intimacy, rather than detracting from spirituality, grows into an increasingly potent expression of a husband and wife's bond, one that is truly body and soul — together.

Looking In for Number One (the Infinite One)

Tzniut cultivates an even more profound relationship.

One of the most intriguing elements of human psychology is the sense that what is hidden is somehow more valuable. In childhood, you were undoubtedly drawn to stories about buried treasures and unexplored islands. You and your best friend shared secrets no one else was privy to. Even now, the fewer people who know about something, the more precious it seems. If you're very spiritual, you may even sense that the unknown seems to whisper of a different world, to beckon you to an existence beyond your own.

What is the source of this almost mystical pull toward the unknown?

God implanted within us a powerful desire for connection to something beyond ourselves — for transcendence. Our attraction to exotic places and pursuits reflects this profound, inarticulate yearning. Its true purpose is to propel us toward the ultimate Mystery — God.

The Talmud (*Shabbat* 133b) counsels that to become close to God, we must activate the divine image within ourselves by becoming more *like* God. As God is merciful, so should we be merciful. As God is giving, so should we be.

God is largely unseen. By choosing to reveal yourself selectively, you mirror God's hiddenness.

Furthermore, God has no divisions; God is One. When our essence permeates everything we do, we unite inside and outside. We, too, become one.

In living *tzniut*, we deepen our relationship not only with ourselves and others, but with the Source of all. In so doing, we convey the essential message of existence: Whatever is most precious and real is less revealed — and we must embrace this hidden dimension of life if we are to restore oneness to ourselves and to the world.

CHAPTER NINE

Being Yourself

Once, after I'd given a class on *tzniut*, a young woman raised her hand, looking disturbed.

"You've said that we're not really our looks, accomplishments, or causes, all of which vary from person to person. Instead, our truest self is our soul, the deepest part of us, which everyone has. So doesn't that mean we're all essentially the same? While *tzniut* makes us spiritual, doesn't it also make us into clones?"

True, because we are all souls, we are all similar. And the more we realize this common denominator, the more we bond with all other souls on the planet — which is beautiful.

At the same time, every soul is different. As I've said, the entire physical world manifests a deeper spiritual reality. That no two human beings are physically identical (even "identical" twins) therefore means they are not *spiritually* identical. As the Mishnah (*Sanhedrin* 4:5) tells us: When a person mints many coins from one mold, they all come out the same; but although God fashions everyone in the mold of the first human, we're each unique.

If each human soul is unique, then affirming you're a soul — which is what *tzniut* is all about — also means affirming your uniqueness. In fact, you express *tzniut* most fully by being yourself.

Contrary to popular belief, Judaism encourages individuality. Rather than arguing the case, I'll let the Torah and traditional Jewish writings speak for themselves.

Back to the Sources

In an article (Hebrew) entitled "'Where Are You?': The Place of Authenticity in Jewish Thought," educators M. Kujawski and D. Nov explore the biblical story of Adam and Eve. After disobeying God by eating from the Tree of Knowledge of Good and Evil, Adam and Eve hide, whereupon God calls to them, "Where are you?" (Genesis 3:8-9). Of course, God knows where they are. What God is asking is: "Where are you *at*?" As a result of their fatal mistake, Adam and Eve are now estranged not only from God but from their own selves. Just as the Hebrew word for "face," *panim*, is plural, the human now has two "faces" — an artificial, external one, and an authentic, internal one. The question "Where are you?" — or, actually, "*Who* are you?" — asks the first man and woman to search for their genuine identity.

Adam and Eve's souls, Judaism teaches, included those of every person who would ever live. God's question therefore reverberates within us all. In asking, "Where are you?"

God invites us to embark upon the intensely individual process of self-discovery.

This search dominates the life of Abraham, the great spiritual seeker. Sending him from his birthplace to the land of Canaan (Genesis 12:1), God doesn't say, "*lech*," "go," but "*lech lecha*" — literally, "go to yourself." Now that you've found and committed yourself to Me, God tells Abraham, you must find yourself, because having a relationship with Me requires you to unearth your own potential.

Abraham and Sarah have a son, Isaac, and he and his wife, Rebecca, have a son Jacob, whose twelve sons lead the Jewish people. At the end of Genesis, Jacob gives each son a different blessing, recognizing that each has his own nature and destiny.

By the beginning of Numbers, the Jews have developed into a nation of twelve tribes. There the Torah describes them and the different flags under which they traveled in the desert, symbolizing each tribe's uniqueness. Finally, it counts the Jewish people's 600,000 core souls, source of untold individual souls throughout history.*

Here's where things get really interesting. The previous Slonimer Rebbe (*Netivot Shalom*, "*BeMidbar*") cites an idea from the Arizal. This 16th-century Kabbalistic genius informs us that, mystically, the four letters of God's name, *yud* and *hei* and *vav* and *hei*, in all their alphabetical and nu-

* For more on the meaning of the 600,000, see Ari D. Kahn, *Explorations: In-Depth Analysis of the Weekly Parashah through the Prism of Rabbinic Perspective*, pp. 307-315.

merical permutations, combine in 600,000 ways. Similarly, the 19th-century *S'fat Emet* of the Ger dynasty ("*BeMidbar*" 5636), quoting another Kabbalistic source, explains that each of the 600,000 souls has its own letter in the Torah — and the Torah is composed entirely of names of God. According to both Chassidic masters, every core soul of the Jewish people corresponds to a different name, or aspect, of God. *S'fat Emet* concludes that each Jew should cleave to the name belonging to him or her. In other words, there are 600,000 ways of relating to God, and we must each find our own.

The mid-20th-century Rabbi Yerucham HaLevi of Mir (*Da'at Chochma U'Mussar*, part 1, p. 188) extends this concept to our relationship with the Torah. The Torah was received, he says, not by the Jewish people, but by each individual Jew, accompanied by his or her own interpretation. Just as the Jewish people comprise 600,000 core souls, there are 600,000 valid interpretations of the Torah, within the parameters the Torah itself sets forth. (Also see the early 17th-century *Shnei Luchot HaBrit*, "*Bereshit*.")

As noted, the number 600,000 refers to core souls, of which there are innumerable offshoots. Each of these also has its unique understanding of the Torah. In Psalms (1:2) we read: "But his delight is in the Torah of the Lord; and in his Torah he meditates day and night." Rashi, the 11th-century biblical commentator, explains that at first, the Torah is God's; but once you work to comprehend it, it becomes yours. The Chafetz Chayim (*Shem Olam*, part 1, ch. 13), an early 20th-century Torah luminary, writes that your own personal share in Torah is a hidden treasure you must find.

The very development of Jewish law requires awareness of and respect for differences among Jews. In an essay entitled "The Daughters of Tzelafchad," Sarah Schneider recounts the story of these five righteous women who, having no brothers, petition Moses for the right to inherit their father's portion in the Land of Israel (Numbers 27:1-11). Moses brings their case before God, who tells him, "The daughters of Tzelafchad speak right," and thus is established a legal precedent for posterity. As Schneider notes, these women revealed part of the Written Torah. Citing Rabbi Tzadok HaCohen, the 19th-century Chassidic master of Ishbitz (*Likutei Ma'amarim*, pp. 80-81; *Yisrael Kedoshim*, p. 152), she explains that, while the Written Torah is now immutable, every Jew — due to the unique circumstances of his or her life — reveals a piece of the Oral Torah: either a new law or, more often, a new application of a pre-existing one. The resulting "unique facet of truth" enriches the body of Jewish wisdom.

According to the 20th-century ethical leader Rabbi Eliyahu Eliezer Dessler (*Michtav Me'Eliyahu*, vol. 1, pp. 22-23), however, the primary beneficiaries of individuality are the individuals themselves. To paraphrase his words:

The purpose of observing *mitzvot* is to sanctify God's name. We do this by overcoming our personal inclinations and performing God's will. This does not benefit God, who needs nothing — it benefits *us*.

However, if a group of people came to honor a mortal king and each made the same speech, one after the other, how would the second speaker feel, and all the more so the last, knowing he or she had added nothing?

God therefore showed us a tremendous kindness in creating us with different natures, strengths, and struggles, so each of us can sanctify God's name in our own unique way. We each therefore have our own special place in the world to come and can rejoice in our reward.

In short, individuality is God's gift to you, allowing you the joy of giving a unique gift in return.

Yet being an individual can be scary. Sometimes we're tempted to flee the challenge and seek shelter in conformity. According to the 18th-century Chassidic commentary *Degel Machane Efrayim* ("*Yitro*," s.v. "*velo*"), the Torah cautions against this human tendency. The second of the Ten Commandments reads (Exodus 20:4): "You shall not make for yourself [*lecha*] any carved idol [*pesel*], or any likeness of any thing...." The word *lecha*, *Degel Machane Efrayim* points out, can be understood as not only "for yourself" (or, as with the command to Abraham, "to yourself") but "*of* yourself." Furthermore, the word *pesel*, "carved idol," is related to *pesolet*, "garbage." Translated this way, the verse reads, "Don't make garbage of yourself"; that is, don't throw away who you are. Likewise, one might add, don't make yourself into "any likeness of any thing" by trying to be someone you're not. In addition to the image of God in which we were created, we each have our own innate makeup, upbringing, education, and society of origin, all of which contribute to our identity. With the Torah's guidance, we must each actualize our Godly image in our own unique way.

Yehudah Sarebnik, in his book *VeNafshi Yoda'at Me'od 2* (published in English as *Secrets of the Soul*; pp. 145-149 in the Hebrew edition), recounts a conversation with a brain-damaged 8-year-old girl that took place through facilitated communication, in which someone supported her hand while she struck computer keys. (Jewish sources suggest, for reasons explained in the book, that the mentally challenged are spiritually more connected than ordinary people.)

This child communicated something deeply insightful. The dialogue revolved around a Jewish man's responsibility to do *chessed* versus his ongoing obligation to study Torah. The girl repeatedly stressed the importance of *chessed*. Her interlocutor asked, "But doesn't the Talmud forbid a Torah scholar to interrupt his study in order to perform a mitzvah someone else can do?"

She replied, "Yes, but if he's a true Torah scholar, he'll know there's *chessed* that only *he* can do." Certain *chessed* is custom-made for you, for you are unique.

Perhaps the most succinct affirmation of Judaism's regard for individuality comes from a revered educator in my neighborhood. When I told her some people believe religious observance means forfeiting one's individuality, she replied, "*God forbid.*"

Every individual is essential to the Jewish people. Just as

a Torah scroll is invalid if even one letter, or part of a letter, is missing or damaged, the Jewish people cannot fulfill its mission if you are not you.

Public and Private Faces

If the Torah wants us to affirm our individuality, why the considerable conformity in dress and behavior in some Jewish communities?

Life has two sides: public and private. Public life requires compromising some of your individuality to unite with others. The uniforms worn by soldiers, football players, firefighters, hospital staff, and students state, "I belong to this group — and right now, that's what matters most." For the same reason, members of social, professional, political, or religious groups often identify with each other by dressing and even acting similarly. For life isn't only about the individual; it's about being part of something greater. Community "membership" is thus an important part of identity.

At the same time, life must include a private refuge in which you can take off your uniform, kick off your shoes, and be fully yourself. That place is home. If in the public arena, individuality takes a back seat to group affiliation, home is where internal identity should come to the fore.

The value Judaism attaches to both public and private realms was evidenced during the terrible drama of the 1994 Nachshon Wachsman kidnapping. This young Israeli soldier was abducted by terrorists who threatened to kill him if their demands were not met by a certain time that Friday night. Everyone knew the army would attempt a rescue. And so we began praying. Thursday night witnessed a mass recitation of Psalms at the Kotel. And Friday afternoon Jewish women throughout Israel and abroad lit an extra Shabbat candle for Nachshon and beseeched God to save him. Tragically, the episode ended with the deaths of both Nachshon and the soldier who led the rescue team.

Communal prayer gatherings, in which everyone repeats the same majestic words at the same time, have awesome power. Yet every Jew's private, personally worded petition to God has a force of its own. Sadly, neither form of prayer reversed the outcome in Nachshon's case. But the Jewish world intuitively understood the need for both.

In my neighborhood, many men dress similarly to assert their membership in the community. But each of them is a world unto himself. Even look-alike rabbis each have their unique personalities, ways of thinking, religious outlooks, and life perspectives (not to mention senses of humor!).

The Feminine Self

This discussion about individuality has particularly strong ramifications for women. Judaism encourages males' group identity. For example, only men must pray publicly with a *minyan*, a quorum of ten adult males. (And men, observant or not, usually adopt greater conformity in dress than women.) Women, on the other hand, represent the private, internal side of life (see chapter 5 of *Head to Heart*), where *tzniut* and its natural expression, individuality, flourish.

Many years ago, religious girls' schools in Jerusalem introduced uniforms. Traditionalist opponents declared them antithetical to femininity. In the end, to ensure appropriate dress, prevent school from becoming a fashion show, and spare poorer girls shame, uniforms were adopted. But they are a necessary evil. Ideally, females don't belong in uniforms.

I recall reading about a group of feminists who formed a social action committee. Had they been men, they undoubtedly would have jumped into the role of "team players," establishing rules of order and planning strategy. But these women chose to spend their first session sharing their thoughts, feelings, and experiences. They coalesced as an effective group only after bonding as individuals. Even feminists are still feminine.

One Plus One

For both sexes, being yourself is essential in marriage. This means, among other things, recognizing whether a traditional masculine or feminine role suits you.

A young woman recently wrote to me:

> I am 23 years old and happily married to a wonderful guy. But I'm not the stereotypical Jewish "wife." I love to learn. While my teachers and rabbis have been encouraging, my peers sometimes tease me about my intellectual curiosity. They don't understand how my love of knowledge brings me closer to God — they think I should cook and keep house in-

> stead. Meanwhile, I am suffering tremendously from not fitting the role I am expected to play. I believe God loves me and created me to be as I am. And I believe my abstract thinking makes me a thoughtful wife and a good mother. Please help everyone see that Jewish women come in all different molds.

Every society has its ideas about who men and women should be. Some women must defend their intellectualism, while others must justify their decision to quit work and be stay-at-home moms. Many men experience similar pressures to conform, whether to a macho or sensitive, "New Age" image.

While Judaism believes men and women are innately different, that doesn't mean all men — or women — are the same. Each of us lies somewhere along a gender continuum. Typically, feminine traits predominate in females and masculine in males, which is why we generalize about women and men. But the balance varies. While affirming your essential gender identity, therefore, affirm your own "mix" of traits as well — ideally before choosing a marriage partner. And once married, know that Jewish law permits a couple to divide responsibilities however they please. (I felt like a failure as a traditional wife until I realized that a different kind of relationship worked for my husband and me.)

Marriage can suffer from resentment or depression when one or both partners forfeit their identities. I recall a highly intelligent friend of mine who had been a spirited, creative, and independent single. Shortly after her wedding, she came over for Shabbat, and I barely recognized her. She was dressed very conservatively, wearing a wig that didn't suit her at all, and sat primly at the table, barely saying a word. "What happened to her?" I wondered.

A few months later she called me, depressed. "Now that I'm a wife," she asked, "who am *I*?" She had been trying to play a role that had little to do with her personality — and needless to say, her depression didn't benefit her marriage. Thankfully, she rediscovered herself: She traded in her wig for colorful scarves, developed a by-women, for-women Jewish comedy show, and with the encouragement of her husband (who, fortunately, appreciated his wife's real self), began writing a book. Her happiness was restored and her marriage strengthened.

When children enter the picture, individuality can take on new dimensions.

A woman I know embarrassedly asked a *rebbetzin* (rabbi's wife) if privately giving her kids "elephant rides" was appropriate for a religious mother. The *rebbetzin* recounted the story of a Sage who would get down on all fours and bark for his children. "In parenting," she concluded with a smile, "you have to be yourself."

It's important that children know their parents not only as members of the community but as individuals.

I know a woman whose son quoted his teacher as having insisted that all Jews should follow Rabbi A. "Hmm...," she responded thoughtfully, "I can see why your teacher would say that. Rabbi A certainly is a great man." A few weeks later, her son asked her what Jewish law said about a certain issue. "Well," she replied casually, "Rabbi A would say such and such; Rabbi B would look at it this way; Rabbi C would have an entirely different view...." Without demonstrating disrespect by directly contradicting his teacher, she subtly conveyed that there's more than one legitimate path in Judaism. She gave her son an important message: One can support a communal institution, such as one's child's school, and still have one's own opinions.

As important as individuality is in parenting, however, a couple must remember that their first "child" is their marriage. And just as it's written (Proverbs 22:6), "Educate the child according to his [or her] way," they must let their marital relationship develop according to *its* way, for it too has its own unique "personality" and destiny.

Affirming the uniqueness of a marriage may mean shifting with time. Roles that worked for you early on may need adjusting after 5, 10, or 15 years, or as your family grows. If the two of you are essentially well-matched, mature, and love each other, you should be able to negotiate the changes (perhaps with outside guidance) and continue building a strong marriage.

Ideally, you and your spouse achieve oneness while each maintaining the individuality so essential to its richness. As I wrote in *Head to Heart*:

> Once you marry and become one... neither of you

> disappears. A 'we' is built on two 'I's, not two nobodies. Who you each continue to be and what you contribute as individuals is what gives your oneness its strength. .... [The] formula [for marriage] is not one plus one equals two, or two halves equal a whole. It's one plus one equals One. It's like overlapping red and blue to create purple and seeing all three colors simultaneously: each of your personalities plus your shared destiny.

Getting Ready

Everything I've said about individuality has obvious bearing on dating.

In dating, there can be strong social pressure to conform to a certain ideal. As a result, some people search for a perfect specimen rather than a person. *Ba'alei teshuva* (those who "returned" to observance as adults) in particular are sometimes insecure in their new religiosity and eager to appear like everyone else as a sign of having "arrived." Readiness for marriage does include being connected to the Jewish world. But it's hard to find your soulmate if you identify more with your religious image than with who you are inside.

A rabbi I know accordingly counsels his students: "Whomever you marry now that you're religious should be someone you would have married before you became religious." He doesn't mean that if you were once seriously involved with a drug addict, now find an observant one! He's referring to the healthy ingredients that make you feel close to someone. For while growing Jewishly should develop your character, it does not change your inherent nature or personality, which are no less important to a relationship than religiosity. After meeting my husband-to-be, my mother told me she could see us together even if we were completely non-observant. So could I.

Your goal in dating, therefore, should not be to impress your date with how well you fit into a certain segment of Jewish society (for example, by interjecting the appropriate Hebrew and Yiddish expressions into your speech). Rather, show your date the individual inside, and look for the same in him or her.

A certain promising scholar sought a wife who would help support the family while he furthered his studies. One very giving woman he dated was enthusiastic about his goals and eager to help him achieve them, but she was nervous about signing on the dotted line. There were so many unknowns: how she'd experience pregnancy; how she'd feel about leaving a baby and/or toddler in childcare several hours a day; whether she could work at home; and whether she'd be too overwhelmed to find time for herself. But the young man couldn't understand these issues. He kept asking why, if she believed in him, she couldn't commit. Such tunnel vision prevents one from seeing the total personhood of another. One's spouse is first and foremost an individual, and individuals often have complex needs and feelings.

Knowing yourself and wanting to know another is therefore essential to recognizing your soulmate. To paraphrase Schneider,* your soulmate has the perfect combination of attributes to complement yours, so the two of you only "fit" when expressing your true selves. "If we try to mimic an archetypal idea that is not the truth of our nature, we actually risk losing our soulmate, whose chemistry will not respond to this artificial scent." This idea applies not only to gender but to all aspects of individuality — personality, lifestyle, values, and more. To find your soulmate, be yourself.

The Light on the Horizon

Conformism plagues parts of the Jewish world today. Understandably concerned about undesirable outside influences, communities sometimes are more restrictive than the letter of the law demands. The result is often greater homogeneity, particularly in *tzniut*. The more superficial the surrounding culture, the more dos and don'ts in religious dress and behavior, and the more alike religious people appear. In the end, *tzniut* can seem to squelch individuality rather than affirm it.

When I sigh about how far we are from the ideal, my husband patiently reminds me, "We're in exile." Only when the Jewish people returns to a natural existence, living in our own land in a society shaped by Jewish values, will reaction disappear. No longer perceived as a compromise with foreign culture, individuality will be appreciated as the flower-

---

* *Kabbalistic Writings on the Nature of Masculine and Feminine*, p. 35. Available at www.amyisrael.co.il/smallvoice.

ing of the Jewish soul, just as *tzniut* is. Until then, we have to live in an imperfect world and quietly seek ways to be ourselves.

This idea leads us to a new perspective on a source I quoted in *Head to Heart*. The 19th-century Chassidic commentator *Ma'or VaShamesh* (on Exodus 15:20) points out a major spiritual difference between our world and the Messianic future. Our world, he explains, is "linear." A line has a beginning and an end, with each point following the previous one and preceding the next. A line therefore symbolizes hierarchy. In our world, we measure ourselves against others, striving to emulate those we perceive as superior. In the future, however, the world will be "circular." A circle has no beginning or end, no "ahead of" or "behind," only points equidistant from a center. So, too, all human souls will be equidistant from God. Rather than comparing, competing, and conforming, we'll define ourselves only by our equal relationship to God. Each soul will be perceived, and perceive itself, as uniquely special.

We haven't yet reached that world, but we can try to bring more of its light into our own. Affirming individuality in a society that often doesn't calls for insight, effort, and sometimes courage. In short, it isn't easy. As someone once joked, "No one can be exactly like me. Sometimes even I have trouble doing it." But both the Jewish people and our own souls are counting on us.

Conclusion

A simple man once wanted to bathe in the public bathhouse, but a grave concern held him back.

"When people are clothed," he reasoned, "it's easy to tell who's who. But at the bathhouse, where we'll all be undressed, how will I tell myself apart from everyone else?"

He thought and thought, until finally he declared, "I know: I'll tie a red string around my big toe, and when I see it, I'll know the one wearing it is I."

So the man tied a red string around his toe and went off to the bathhouse. Upon arriving, he confidently undressed. Unnoticed, however, the red string slipped off his toe and onto someone else's.

Upon realizing his red string was missing, the simpleton was most distressed. Looking around in desperation, he sighted it on the toe of another and hurried over to him.

> "Excuse me," the simple man said anxiously. "I know who you are, but could you please tell me — who am I?"

This Jewish folktale describes a classic dilemma. For years, we identify ourselves by something external — a "red string." Only when we lose it do we finally confront the difficult and painful question: "Who am I?"

An "identity crisis" is a golden opportunity to journey towards the answer. Yet the path before us is strewn with obstacles. The body/soul split has grown so severe that many consider it completely natural for one to operate independently of the other. Advertisers promote sex appeal and glamorous vacations as the key to happiness. Television, inherently biased toward the superficial, has ravaged our perception of subtlety and depth. And social pressure keeps us fixated on externalities, making it difficult to muster the strength to choose a different path.

Something essential is disintegrating. As a well-known poet wrote of our generation, "things fall apart, the center does not hold." For if the center of the world is to hold, we must first have a strong hold on our own centers.

Given these challenges, *tzniut* doesn't always come easily. A friend summed it up with a sigh: "*Tzniut* is a lost art." *Tzniut* is indeed an art, and few today have mastered it. But it needn't be lost. Each of us — perhaps with the right teacher — can learn to paint our own canvas.

But *tzniut* is ultimately more. For just as an artist's vision eventually colors his or her perception of the world, *tzniut* colors everything we do. *It is a way of life*. And it's acquired not overnight but over time, with awareness, motivation, and practice. *Tzniut* is not black and white; it's a continuum. We can always go further, and every step counts. At any moment, in any situation, we can stop and ask ourselves, "Am I being true to myself?" And little by little, by "trying on" more and more of an internal approach to living, we can grow into the selves we were created to be.

Afterword

The Jewish people were created to be a "light unto the nations" — and when we fail in our mission, we suffer. Today, remiss in numerous areas, we are beset by troubles, including terrorism and other forms of anti-Semitism from without, and alienation and erosion from within.

At the same time, the Torah tells us (Deuteronomy 23:15): "For the Lord your God walks in the midst of your camp, to deliver you and give up your enemies before you; therefore shall your camp be holy: that He see no nakedness in you and turn away from you." The opposite of holiness, what drives God away, is nakedness; its remedy is *tzniut*.

Tzniut offers divine protection. For *tzniut* means not only covering our bodies but gradually piercing through our external layers to the Godliness at our core. God then reciprocates: "Whenever you walk with God in privacy, God will be with you in privacy" (*Tanna DeVei Eliyahu Rabba* 28). The more we turn towards God by defining ourselves internally, the more God turns towards us.

Nowhere is this truer than in the Land of Israel, "a land that fosters the growth of *tzniut*" and embraces those who possess it. The men of the desert generation couldn't appreciate the Land, for they had succumbed to immorality and other foreign values. The Israelites therefore had to wander 40 years, during which all the men died. Only the women, who never abandoned *tzniut*, were privileged to enter the Land they loved (*Kli Yakar*, Numbers 26:64).

Tzniut may not be a panacea for all our troubles, but it's key in turning things around. Long ago, the prophet Micah (6:8) reminded us, "God has told you, humanity, what is good; and what does the Lord require of you but to do justly, love kindness, and walk in *tzniut* with your God." Justice and kindness characterize any enlightened society, but *tzniut* heightens their spirituality immeasurably. Perhaps for this reason, our Sages (*Pesikta Rabbati* 46) teach that nothing is more beloved to God than *tzniut*. And not only in public, but "with your God" — in our private relationship with God.

The more difficult an act, the greater its reward. In our generation, *tzniut* is a tremendous challenge. May we meet the challenge, and merit tremendous blessing.

About the Author

Gila Manolson (née Marilyn Fisch) grew up in the northeastern United States and graduated magna cum laude from Yale University with a degree in music. She later studied at Neve Yerushalayim College for Women. For five years, she was the resident supervisor of the women's branch of Heritage House, a Jewish youth hostel in Jerusalem's Old City. She has taught in numerous programs and is a popular lecturer in Israel and abroad. She is also the author of *The Magic Touch: A Jewish Approach to Relationships* and *Head to Heart: What to Know Before Dating and Marriage*. She and her husband live in Jerusalem with their seven children.